Mastering The Plant-Based Diet

Everything You Need To Know About Plant Based Diet For Beginners, To Build Their Muscles, Lose Weight And Improve Their Overall Health

Ember Erickson

Table of Contents

Introduction

A plant-based diet is a diet based primarily on whole plant foods. It is identical to the regular diet we're used to already, except that it leaves out foods that are not exclusively from plants. Hence, a plant-based diet does away with all types of animal-sourced foods, hydrogenated oils, refined sugars, and processed foods. A whole food plant-based diet comprises not just fruits and vegetables; it also consists of unprocessed or barely processed oils with healthy monounsaturated fats (like extra-virgin olive oil), whole grains, legumes (essentially lentils and beans), seeds and nuts, as well as herbs and spices.

Why You Ought to Reduce Your Intake of Processed and Animal-Based Foods

You have likely heard over and over that processed food has adverse effects on your health. You might have also been told repeatedly to stay away from foods with lots of preservatives; nevertheless, nobody ever offered any genuine or concrete facts about why you ought to avoid these foods and why they are unsafe. Consequently, let us properly dissect it to help you properly comprehend why you ought to stay away from these healthy eating offenders.

They have massive habit-forming characteristics

Humans have a predisposition towards being addicted to some specific foods; however, the reality is that the fault is not wholly ours.

Every one of the unhealthy treats we relish now and then triggers the dopamine release in our brains. This creates a pleasurable effect in our brain, but the excitement is usually short-lived. The discharged dopamine additionally causes an attachment connection gradually, and this is the reason some people consistently go back to eat certain unhealthy foods even when they know it's unhealthy and unnecessary. You can get rid of this by taking out that inducement completely.

They are sugar-laden and plenteous in glucose-fructose syrup

Animal-based and processed foods are laden with refined sugars and glucose-fructose syrup which has almost no beneficial food nutrient. An ever-increasing number of studies are affirming what several people presumed from the start; that genetically modified foods bring about inflammatory bowel disease, which consequently makes it increasingly difficult for the body to assimilate essential nutrients. The disadvantages that result from your body being unable to assimilate essential nutrients from consumed foods rightly cannot be overemphasized.

Processed and animal-based food products contain plenteous amounts of refined carbohydrates. Indeed, your body requires carbohydrates to give it the needed energy to run body capacities.

In any case, refining carbs dispenses with the fundamental supplements; in the way that refining entire grains disposes of the whole grain part. What remains, in the wake of refining, is what's considered as empty carbs or empty calories. These can negatively affect the metabolic system in your body by sharply increasing your blood sugar and insulin quantities.

They contain lots of synthetic ingredients

At the point when your body is taking in non-natural ingredients, it regards them as foreign substances. Your body treats them as a health threat. Your body isn't accustomed to identifying synthetic compounds like sucralose or these synthesized sugars. Hence, in defense of your health against this foreign "aggressor," your body does what it's capable of to safeguard your health. It sets off an immune reaction to tackle this "enemy" compound, which indirectly weakens your body's general disease alertness, making you susceptible to illnesses. The concentration and energy expended by your body in ensuring your immune system remains safe could instead be devoted somewhere else.

They contain constituent elements that set off an excitable reward sensation in your body

A part of processed and animal-based foods contain compounds like glucose-fructose syrup, monosodium glutamate, and specific food dyes that can trigger some addiction. They rouse your body to receive a benefit in return whenever you consume them. Monosodium glutamate, for example, is added to many store-bought baked foods. This additive slowly conditions your palates to relish the taste. It gets mental just by how your brain interrelates with your taste sensors.

This reward-centric arrangement makes you crave it increasingly, which ends up exposing you to the danger of overconsuming calories

For animal protein, usually, the expression "subpar" is used to allude to plant proteins since they generally have lower levels of essential amino acids as against animal-sourced protein. Nevertheless, what the vast majority don't know is that large amounts of essential amino acids can prove detrimental to your health. Let me break it down further for you.

Animal-Sourced Protein has no Fiber

In their pursuit to consume animal protein increasingly, the vast majority wind up dislodging the plant protein that was previously available in their body. Replacing the plant proteins with its animal variant is wrong because, in contrast to plant protein, animal proteins typically have fiber deficiency, phytonutrients, and antioxidant properties. Fiber insufficiency is a regular feature across various regions and societies on the planet. In America, for example, according to the National Academy of Medicine, the typical adult takes in roughly 15 grams of dietary fiber daily rather than the recommended daily quantity of 25 to 30 grams. A deficiency in dietary fiber often leads to a heightened risk of breast and colorectal cancers, in addition to constipation, inflammatory bowel disease, and cardiovascular disease.

Animal Protein Leads to a Jump in IGF-1 Levels

Insulin-like growth factor 1 (IGF-1) is a vital growth hormone identical in molecular geometry to insulin which contributes significantly to the growth of children and impacts adults in an anabolic manner. It fuels cell division and development, which may seemingly seem positive; however, it correspondingly triggers the development of cancer cells. Hence, an increased level of IGF-1 in the blood is connected to a heightened risk of cancer, malignant tumor, and spread.

Animal protein brings about an upsurge in Phosphorus levels in the body

Animal protein has significant levels of Phosphorus. Our bodies stabilize these plenteous amounts of Phosphorus by producing and discharging a hormone known as fibroblast growth factor 23 (FGF23). Studies have shown that this hormone is dangerous to our veins. FGF23 also causes asymmetrical expansion of heart muscles – a determinant for congestive heart failure and even mortality in some advanced cases.

Chapter 1: Breakfast

1. Small Sweet Potato Pancakes

Preparation Time: 20 minutes | **Cooking Time:** 0 minutes | **Servings:** 2

Ingredients:

1 clove of garlic 3 tablespoon wholemeal rice flour

1 pinch of nutmeg 3 tablespoons of water

150 g sweet potato

1 pinch of chili flakes

1 teaspoon oil

Salt

Directions:

Peel the garlic clove and mash it with a fork. Peel the sweet potato and grate it into small sticks with a grater.

Knead the sweet potato and garlic in a bowl with the rice flour and water, then season with chili flakes, salt, and nutmeg.

Heat the oil in a pan and form small buffers.

Fry these in the pan on both sides until golden brown.

Goes perfectly with tzatziki and other fresh dips.

Nutrition:

Calories: 209 Fat: 15.4g Carbs: 10.5g Protein: 8.1g Fiber: 3.2g

2. Tomato and Pesto Toast

Preparation: 5 minu | **Cooking:** 0 minute | **Servings:** 4

Ingredients:

1 small tomato, sliced ¼ teaspoon ground black pepper

1 tablespoon vegan pesto 2 tablespoons hummus

1 slice of whole-grain bread, toasted

Hemp seeds as needed for garnishing

Directions:

Spread hummus on one side of the toast, top with tomato slices and then drizzle with pesto.

Sprinkle black pepper on the toast along with hemp seeds and then serve straight away.

Nutrition:

Calories: 214 Cal Fat: 7.2 g Carbs: 32 g Protein: 6.5 g Fiber: 3 g

3. Avocado and Sprout Toast

Preparation Time: 5 minutes | **Cooking Time:** 0 minute | **Servings:** 4

Ingredients:

1/2 of a medium avocado, sliced

1 slice of whole-grain bread, toasted

2 tablespoons sprouts

2 tablespoons hummus

¼ teaspoon lemon zest

½ teaspoon hemp seeds

¼ teaspoon red pepper flakes

Directions:

Spread hummus on one side of the toast and then top with avocado slices and sprouts.

Sprinkle with lemon zest, hemp seeds, and red pepper flakes, and then serve straight away.

Nutrition:

Calories: 200 Cal Fat: 10.5 g Carbs: 22 g Protein: 7 g Fiber: 7 g

Chapter 2: Main Dishes

4. Eggplant Teriyaki Bowls

Preparation Time: 10-75 minutes | **Cooking Time:** 45

minutes | **Servings:** 4

Ingredients:

1 carrot, shredded

1 chunky eggplant

¼ cup edamame beans, frozen

1 lime, ½ sliced, ½ juiced

2 spring onions, chopped

1 ½ tablespoon vegetable oil

1 handful radishes, sliced

1 tablespoon caster sugar

1 garlic clove, crushed

½ cup jasmine rice

2 tablespoons sesame seeds, toasted

1 small ginger, grated

2 tablespoons soy sauce

Directions:

Add 2 cups of water to a cooking pan, add rice and salt to taste. Bring to a boil, cook for a minute, and then close the lid. Reduce the heat to low and cook for 10 minutes until cooked through. Turn off the heat and steam for an additional 10 minutes.

Add a tablespoon of oil to a bowl and toss the eggplant in it. Preheat the wok pan, add the eggplant, and cook for 5 minutes, stirring often, until slightly softened and charred. Add the carrots to the wok along with garlic, ginger, and spring onions, and then fry for 2-3 minutes. In a small bowl, whisk the sugar along with soy sauce and a cup of water, and then add it into the wok. Simmer until the eggplant is very soft, for about 10-15 minutes. Add water to the pan and bring to a boil and then add the frozen edamame beans, remove the beans, drain and rinse them well under running water. Add the radishes to a bowl, drain the beans again, and then add them to the radishes. Squeeze lime juice on top and toss well until combined.

Serve the rice in the bowls and then scoop the eggplant and sauce on top along with the beans and radishes.

Sprinkle with sesame seeds and garnish with the lime slices. Enjoy

Nutrition:

Calories: 140 Cal Fat: 0.9 g Carbs: 27.1 g Protein: 6.3 g

Fiber: 6.2 g

5. Quinoa and Black Bean Chilli

Preparation Time: 10-75 minutes | **Cooking Time:** 45 minutes | **Servings:** 8

Ingredients:

3 cups vegetable stock

1 onion, chopped

1 cup quinoa, rinsed, drained

1 red chili, chopped

2 teaspoons ground cumin

1 lb. tomatoes, chopped

olive oil spray

1 teaspoon smoked paprika

1 small avocado, sliced

½ teaspoon chili powder

2 garlic cloves, crushed

1 lb. black beans, rinsed, drained

Coriander leaves, to serve

Directions:

Generously grease the cooking pan with oil and place over medium heat and then add the onion, red chili, and garlic. Fry the ingredients until soft, and then add spices and stir.

Add the vegetable stock into the pan along with quinoa, black beans, and tomatoes, and then adjust the seasonings if needed.

Close the lid and simmer until quinoa is tender, for about 30 minutes.

When done, garnish with coriander leaves and top with the avocado slices. Serve and enjoy!

Nutrition:

Calories: 140 Cal Fat: 0.9 g Carbs: 27.1 g Protein: 6.3 g Fiber: 6.2 g

6. Broccoli Mac and Cheese

Preparation Time: 10-75 minutes | **Cooking Time:** 20 minutes | **Servings:** 4

Ingredients:

8 oz. whole-grain macaroni elbows, cooked

1 head of broccoli, florets

1 ½ tablespoon avocado oil

1 onion, chopped

1 cup potato, peeled and grated

3 cloves garlic, minced

½ teaspoon garlic powder

½ teaspoon onion powder

½ teaspoon dry mustard powder

1 small pinch of red pepper flakes

⅔ cup raw cashews

1 cup water, or more if needed

¼ cup nutritional yeast

3 teaspoons apple cider vinegar

salt

Directions:

Place a large pot over medium heat. Add salt and water and bring to a boil.

Add broccoli and cook for 5 minutes. Once done, drain excess liquid and set aside in a large mixing bowl.

Place a large skillet over medium heat. Add oil.

Add onion, salt and cook for about 5 minutes.

Add potatoes, garlic, garlic powder, onion powder, mustard powder, salt, red pepper flakes and cook for 60 seconds.

Add cashews, water, bring the mixture to a simmer, reduce the heat, and let it cook until potatoes are tender. Remove from the heat.

Pour the mixture into a food processor, add nutritional yeast, vinegar, and pulse until the mixture is smooth, adding water if necessary.

Serve cooked pasta in bowls, topped with the blended mixture.

Nutrition:

Calories:680, Total Fat:71.8g, Saturated Fat:20.9g, Total Carbs:10g, Dietary Fiber:7g, Sugar:2g, Protein:3g, Sodium:525mg

7. Butternut Squash Linguine with Fried Sage

Preparation Time: 10-75 minutes | **Cooking Time:** 25 minutes | **Servings:** 4

Ingredients:

3 cups butternut squash, peeled, seeded, and chopped

2 cups vegetable broth

12 oz. whole-grain fettuccine, cooked, 1 cup cooking liquid saved 1 onion, chopped

2 garlic cloves, pressed

2 tablespoons olive oil

1 tablespoon fresh sage, chopped

⅛ teaspoon red pepper flakes

salt and pepper

Directions:

Place a large pan over medium heat. Add oil.

Add sage and cook it until crispy. Season with salt and set aside.

Return the same pan to medium heat, add butternut, onion, garlic, red pepper flakes, salt, and pepper. Cook for about 10 minutes.

Add broth and bring to a boil, then reduce the heat and let it cook for 20 minutes.

Place a pot of salty water over medium heat.

Cool the squash mixture and blend the mixture until smooth with a mixer.

Add pasta, ¼ cup reserved pasta liquid to the pan, return pan to medium heat and cook for 3 minutes.

Nutrition:

Calories: 140 Cal Fat: 0.9 g Carbs: 27.1 g Protein: 6.3 g Fiber: 6.2 g

8. Paella

Preparation Time: 10-75 minutes | **Cooking Time:** 1 hour | **Servings:** 6

Ingredients:

15 oz. diced tomatoes, drained

2 cups short-grain brown rice

1 ½ cups cooked chickpeas

3 cups vegetable broth

⅓ cup dry white wine

1 14 oz. artichokes, drained and chopped

½ cup Kalamata olives pitted and halved

¼ cup parsley, chopped

½ cup peas

3 tablespoons extra-virgin olive oil, divided

1 onion, chopped

6 garlic cloves, pressed or minced

2 teaspoons smoked paprika

½ teaspoon saffron threads, crumbled

2 bell peppers, stemmed, seeded, and sliced

2 tablespoons lemon juice

salt and pepper

Directions:

Preheat the oven to 350F.

Place a large skillet over medium heat and add 2 tablespoons of oil.

Add onion, salt and cook for 5 minutes.

Add garlic, paprika and cook for ½ a minute.

Add tomatoes and stir well. Cook until the mixture starts to thicken.

Add rice and cook for 1 minute while stirring.

Add chickpeas, broth, wine, saffron, and salt to taste. Increase the heat and bring the mixture to a boil. Remove from the heat.

Cover and immediately transfer to an oven on the lower rack. Bake for 1 hour.

Prepare a baking sheet by lining it with parchment paper. Combine artichokes, peppers, olives, 1 tablespoon olive oil, salt, and pepper. Mix well and roast vegetables on the upper rack in the oven for 45 minutes.

Add parsley and lemon juice to the baking pan and mix well.

Sprinkle the roasted vegetables and peas on the baked rice.

Nutrition:

Calories: 140 Cal Fat: 0.9 g Carbs: 27.1 g Protein: 6.3 g Fiber: 6.2 g

9. Spicy Thai Peanut Sauce Over Roasted Sweet Potatoes and Rice

Preparation Time: 10-75 minutes | **Cooking Time:** 1 hour 30 minutes | **Servings:** 4

Ingredients:

For the spicy Thai peanut sauce:

½ cup creamy peanut butter

¼ cup reduced-sodium tamari

3 tablespoons apple cider vinegar

2 tablespoons honey or maple syrup

1 teaspoon grated fresh ginger

2 cloves garlic, pressed

¼ teaspoon red pepper flakes

2 tablespoons water

For the roasted vegetables:

2 sweet potatoes, peeled and sliced

1 bell pepper, cored, deseeded, and sliced

about 2 tablespoons coconut oil (or olive oil)

¼ teaspoon cumin powder

salt

For the rice and garnishes:

1 ¼ cup jasmine brown rice

2 green onions, sliced

a handful of cilantro, torn

a handful of peanuts, crushed

Directions:

Place a pot of water on medium heat and bring it to a boil. Preheat the oven to 425F.

On a rimmed baking sheet, mix sweet potato, 1 tablespoon coconut oil, cumin, and salt. Roast in the middle rack for about 35 minutes.

On another baking sheet, mix bell pepper with 1 teaspoon coconut oil, salt and mix well, Roast on the top rack for about 20 minutes until tender.

When water is boiling in the pot add rice and mix well. Cook for about 30 minutes and drain excess liquid. Once done, cover and let it sit for 10 minutes, fluff it after.

Mix sauce ingredients in a small bowl and set aside.

Divide rice, roasted vegetables in bowls and top with sauce, green onions, cilantro, and peanuts before serving.

Nutrition:

Calories:680, Total Fat:71.8g, Saturated Fat:20.9g, Total Carbs:10g, Dietary Fiber:7g, Sugar:2g, Protein:3g, Sodium:525mg

10. Butternut Squash Chipotle Chili With Avocado

Preparation Time: 10-75 minutes | **Cooking Time:** 20 minutes | **Servings:** 4

Ingredients:

3 cups black beans, cooked

14 oz. can diced tomatoes, including the liquid

2 cups vegetable broth

1 onion, chopped

2 bell peppers, chopped

1 small butternut squash, cubed

4 garlic cloves, minced

2 tablespoons olive oil

1 tablespoon chili powder

½ tablespoon chopped chipotle pepper in adobo

1 teaspoon ground cumin

¼ teaspoon ground cinnamon

1 bay leaf

2 avocados, diced

3 corn tortillas for crispy tortilla strips

salt

Directions:

Place a stockpot over medium heat. Add oil.

Add and cook onion, bell peppers, and butternut squash for about 5 minutes.

Reduce the heat, add garlic, chili powder, ½ tablespoon chopped chipotle peppers, cumin, and cinnamon. Cook for ½ a minute.

Add bay leaves, black beans, tomatoes, and their juices and broth. Mix well. Cook for about 1 hour. Remove bay leaf when done cooking.

Slice corn tortillas into thin little strips.

Place a pan over medium heat and add olive oil. Add tortilla strips and season with salt. Cook until crispy for about 7 minutes. Remove from the heat and place in a bowl covered with a paper towel to drain excess oil.

Serve chili in bowls, topped with crispy tortilla chips and avocado.

Nutrition:

Calories: 140 Cal Fat: 0.9 g Carbs: 27.1 g Protein: 6.3 g Fiber: 6.2 g

11. Chickpea Biryani

Preparation Time: 10-75 minutes | **Cooking Time:** 40 minutes | **Servings:** 6

Ingredients:

4 cups veggie stock

2 cups basmati rice, rinsed

1 can chickpeas, drained, rinsed

½ cup raisins

1 large onion, thinly sliced

2 cups thinly sliced veggies (bell pepper, zucchini, and carrots)

3 garlic cloves, chopped

1 tablespoon ginger, chopped

1 tablespoon cumin

1 tablespoon coriander

1 teaspoon chili powder

1 teaspoon cinnamon

½ teaspoon cardamom

½ teaspoon turmeric

2 tablespoons olive oil

1 bay leaf

salt

Directions:

Place a large skillet over medium-high heat. Add oil.

Sauté onions for about 5 minutes.

Reduce the heat to medium, add vegetables, garlic, and ginger. Cook for 5 minutes. Scoop 1 cup of this mixture and set aside.

Add spices, bay leaf, and rice. Stir for about 1 minute.

Add stock and salt to taste.

Add chickpeas, raisins, and 1 cup of vegetables. Bring the mixture to a simmer over high heat.

Lower the heat, cover tightly, and let it simmer for ½ an hour. Remove from the heat when rice is done.

Nutrition:

Calories: 140 Cal Fat: 0.9 g Carbs: 27.1 g Protein: 6.3 g Fiber: 6.2 g

12. Chinese Eggplant

Preparation Time: 10-75 minutes | **Cooking Time:** 45 minutes | **Servings:** 4

Ingredients:

1 ½ lbs. eggplants, chopped

2 cups of water

2 tablespoons cornstarch

4 tablespoons peanut oil

4 cloves garlic, chopped

2 teaspoons ginger, minced

10 dried red chilies

salt

For the Szechuan sauce:

1 teaspoon Szechuan peppercorns

¼ cup of soy sauce

1 tablespoon garlic chili paste

1 tablespoon sesame oil

1 tablespoon rice vinegar

1 tablespoon Chinese cooking wine

3 tablespoons coconut sugar

½ teaspoon five-spice

Directions:

Place chopped eggplants in a shallow bowl. Add water and 2 teaspoons of salt. Stir cover and let it sit for about 15 minutes.

Meanwhile, place a small pan over medium heat. Toast the Szechuan peppercorns for about 2 minutes and crush them.

Add crushed peppercorns to a medium bowl, add soy, chili paste, sesame oil, rice vinegar, Chinese cooking vinegar, coconut sugar, and five spices.

Drain excess liquid from the eggplants and toss in the corn starch.

Place a large skillet over medium heat, add eggplants and cook them until golden. Set aside.

Add 1 tablespoon of oil to the skillet placed over medium heat. Cook garlic and ginger for 2 minutes.

Add dried chilies and cook for 1 minute. Add the Szechuan sauce and bring the mixture to a simmer in 20 seconds.

Add back eggplants and cook for about 60 seconds.

Nutrition:

Calories:680, Total Fat:71.8g, Saturated Fat:20.9g, Total Carbs:10g, Dietary Fiber:7g, Sugar:2g, Protein:3g, Sodium:525mg

13. Black Pepper Tofu with Bok Choy

Preparation Time: 10-75 minutes | **Cooking Time:** 30 minutes | **Servings:** 2

Ingredients:

12 oz. firm tofu, cubed 1/3 cup cornstarch for dredging

2 tablespoons coconut oil

1 teaspoon freshly cracked peppercorns

1 shallot, sliced 4 cloves garlic, chopped

6 oz. baby bok choy, sliced into 4 slices

For the black pepper sauce:

2 tablespoons soy sauce

2 tablespoons Chinese cooking wine

2 tablespoons water

1 teaspoon brown sugar

½ teaspoon freshly cracked peppercorns

1 teaspoon chili paste

Directions:

In a small bowl, combine wok sauce ingredients and mix well until sugar dissolves. Set aside.

Place cornstarch in a shallow bowl and dredge tofu in the cornstarch. Set aside.

Place a large skillet over medium heat. Heat 1 tablespoon coconut oil.

Add peppercorns and toast for about 1 minute.

Add tofu and cook on all sides for about 6 minutes. Set tofu aside.

Add the remaining coconut oil. Add shallots, garlic, and bok choy. Cook for 8 minutes.

Add back the tofu and cook for less than a minute.

Nutrition:

Calories: 140 Cal Fat: 0.9 g Carbs: 27.1 g Protein: 6.3 g Fiber: 6.2 g

14.   Spaghetti Alla Puttanesca

Preparation Time: 10-75 minutes | **Cooking Time:** 30 minutes | **Servings:** 4

Ingredients:

For the Puttanesca sauce:

28 oz. can chunky tomato sauce

⅓ cup chopped Kalamata olives

⅓ cup capers

1 tablespoon Kalamata olive brine

1 tablespoon caper brine

3 cloves garlic, minced

¼ teaspoon red pepper flakes

1 tablespoon olive oil

½ cup parsley leaves, chopped and divided

salt and pepper

For the pasta:

8 oz. whole-grain spaghetti

6 oz. zucchini noodles

Directions:

Place a medium skillet over medium heat.

Add tomato sauce, olives, capers, olive brine, caper brine, garlic, and red pepper flakes. Bring the mixture to a boil, reduce the heat, and let it simmer for 20 minutes. Remove from the heat and set aside.

Place a pot over medium heat. Add water, salt, spaghetti, and cook as directed on the package. When done, drain excess water.

Pour the sauce over pasta and mix well.

Add zucchini noodles before serving.

Nutrition:

Calories: 140 Cal Fat: 0.9 g Carbs: 27.1 g Protein: 6.3 g Fiber: 6.2 g

15.   Thai Red Curry

Preparation Time: 10-75 minutes | **Cooking Time:** 40 minutes | **Servings:** 4

Ingredients:

1 ¼ cups brown jasmine rice, rinsed

1 tablespoon coconut oil 1 cup onion, chopped

1 tablespoon fresh ginger, ginger

2 cloves garlic, minced 1 red bell pepper, sliced

1 yellow bell pepper, sliced

3 carrots, peeled and sliced

2 tablespoons Thai red curry paste

1 14 oz. can coconut milk

½ cup of water 1 ½ cups packed kale, chopped

1 ½ teaspoon coconut sugar

1 tablespoon tamari

2 teaspoons fresh lime juice

Directions:

Place a large pot over medium heat and add water. Bring it to a boil.

Add rice, salt and cook for 30 minutes. Remove from the heat, cover, and let it sit for 10 minutes.

Place a large pan over medium heat. Add oil.

Cook onion and salt for about 5 minutes.

Add garlic, ginger and cook for about ½ a minute.

Add bell peppers, carrots and cook for about 5 minutes.

Add curry paste and cook for an additional 2 minutes.

Add coconut milk, water, kale, sugar, tamari, and lime juice. Remove from the heat.

Nutrition:

Calories:680, Total Fat:71.8g, Saturated Fat:20.9g, Total Carbs:10g, Dietary Fiber:7g, Sugar:2g, Protein:3g, Sodium:525mg

16.   Salisbury Steak and Mushroom Gravy

Preparation Time: 30 minutes | **Cooking Time:** 30-120 minutes | **Servings:** 4

Ingredients:

4 palm-sized pieces of beef seitan

1 1/2 tablespoons vegan chicken-flavored bouillon

8 ounces mushrooms, chopped

1/2 teaspoon garlic powder

1/2 teaspoon basil

1 bay leaf

1/8 teaspoon celery salt

1/8 teaspoon seasoned salt

1/4 teaspoon pepper

1 cup of water

1 cup non-dairy milk

2 tablespoons olive oil

1/2 cup plus 3 tablespoons flour

Directions:

Make a coating for the seitan by mixing the garlic powder, celery salt, ½ cup flour, basil, seasoned salt, and pepper in a bowl. Make sure the seitan is wet before coating it with the flour mixture.

Heat the oil in the instant pot on the sauté setting. Brown the seitan steaks on each side, then set aside.

Add the water, mushrooms, bay leaf, and bouillon to the instant pot, then place the seitan on top. Seal the lid and cook on high for 4 minutes, before letting the pressure release naturally.

Remove the lid and discard the bay leaf. Return to the sauté setting.

Remove the steaks, then stir in the non-dairy milk. Add the flour to thicken the gravy, then add the steaks. Simmer for 10 minutes. Add additional flour if needed. Serve with a side of mashed potatoes smothered in your mushroom gravy.

Nutrition:

Calories: 140 Cal Fat: 0.9 g Carbs: 27.1 g Protein: 6.3 g Fiber: 6.2 g

17. Stuffed Sweet Onions

Preparation Time: 45 minutes | **Cooking Time:** 30-120 minutes | **Servings:** 5

Ingredients:

10 medium-sized sweet onions

1 lb portobello mushrooms, chopped

1 medium-sized eggplant, finely chopped

3 tbsp olive oil

1 tbsp dried mint

1 tsp cayenne pepper

½ tsp cumin powder

1 tsp salt

½ cup tomato paste

¼ cup fresh parsley, finely chopped

Directions:

Cut a ¼-inch slice from the top of each onion and trim a small amount from the bottom end. This will make the onions stand upright. Place onions in a microwave-safe dish and add about 1 cup of water. Cover with a tight lid and microwave on High for 2-3 minutes. Remove onions from a dish and cool slightly. Now carefully remove the inner layers of onions with a sharp knife, leaving about a ¼-inch onion shell.

In a large bowl, combine chopped mushrooms, eggplant, olive oil, mint, cayenne pepper, cumin powder, salt, and tomato paste. Use 1 tablespoon of the mixture to fill the onions.

Grease the bottom of the stainless steel insert with some oil and gently place onions. Add 2 cups of water or vegetable stock and seal the lid. Press the 'Manual' button and set the timer for 15 minutes.

When done, release the pressure naturally and open the lid. Sprinkle with parsley before serving.

Nutrition:

Calories: 140 Cal Fat: 0.9 g Carbs: 27.1 g Protein: 6.3 g Fiber: 6.2 g

18. Lemony Roasted Vegetable Risotto

Preparation Time: 30 minutes | **Cooking Time:** 15-120 minutes | **Servings:** 4

Ingredients:

3 1/2 Cups Butternut Squash, peeled, cubed

1/1/2 Cups Zucchini, diced

1 large Carrot, peeled, chopped

2 Tablespoons Olive Oil

Sea Salt + Pepper to taste

1 Onion, diced

2 Garlic Cloves, minced

6 cups Vegetable Broth

1 Tablespoon Vegan Butter

2 cups Arborio Rice

1/2 Cup Baby Spinach

1 Teaspoon Lemon Zest

2 Tablespoons lemon juice, more to taste

Directions:

Preheat the oven to 400 degrees F. Line a baking tray with parchment paper. Add butternut squash, zucchini, and carrot to the tray. Coat with 1 teaspoon of olive oil, salt, and pepper, toss well.

Roast in the oven for 15-20 minutes or until squash is soft when poked with a fork. When done, remove from the oven and set aside.

Press saute mode on the instant pot. Add remaining olive oil, and when hot, cook onions and garlic for 2-3 minutes or until onions become semi-transparent.

Add rice and stir for 1-2 minutes to coat.

Add broth, and vegan butter. Stir to combine.

Turn the instant pot off. Cover and seal. Press the manual button and adjust the time to 7 minutes.

When done cooking, release the pressure and stir well.

Return to saute mode, add spinach and roasted vegetables.

Stir until the spinach has wilted. Taste and add salt and pepper as needed.

Top with lemon juice and zest.

Best when served fresh and warm.

Enjoy!

Nutrition:

Calories: 140 Cal Fat: 0.9 g Carbs: 27.1 g Protein: 6.3 g Fiber: 6.2 g

Chapter 3: Side Dishes

19. Three-Bean Chili

Preparation Time: 10 minutes | **Cooking Time:** 30 minutes | **Servings:** 2

Ingredients:

¼ cup dried pinto beans soaked 8 hours or overnight

¼ cup dried kidney beans soaked 8 hours or overnight

¼ cup dried black beans soaked 8 hours or overnight

½ tablespoon olive oil

1 small onion chopped

1 teaspoon salt

½ tablespoon tomato paste

½ teaspoon garlic powder

1 teaspoon paprika

1 teaspoon cumin powder

½ teaspoon coriander powder

½ cup crushed tomatoes 1 can

2 cups of water

Chopped fresh cilantro

Directions:

Drain and rinse beans. Press Sauté; to the Instant Pot.

Cook for 3 to 4 minutes. Remove to a bowl.

Heat olive oil in Instant Pot. Add onion, cook, and stir for

3 minutes or until softened. Add salt, tomato paste,

garlic powder, paprika, cumin powder, and coriander powder; cook and stir for 1 minute. Stir in tomatoes, water, beans; mix well.

Secure lid and move pressure release valve to sealing position. Press Manual or Pressure Cook; cook at High pressure 20 minutes.

When cooking is complete, use Natural-release for 10 minutes, then release remaining pressure. Garnish with cilantro.

Nutrition:

Calories 120, Total Fat 4. 1g, Saturated Fat 0. 6g, Cholesterol 0mg, Sodium 1221mg, Total Carbohydrate 22. 4g, Dietary Fiber 10g, Total Sugars 2. 8g, Protein 7. 4g

20. Broccoli and Black Bean Chili

Preparation Time: 15 minutes | **Cooking Time:** 15 minutes | **Servings:** 2

Ingredients:

½ tablespoon coconut oil

1 cup broccoli

1 cup chopped red onions

½ tablespoon paprika

1/2 teaspoon salt ¼ cup tomatoes

1 cup black beans drained, rinsed

¼ chopped green chills

½ cup of water

Directions:

In the Instant Pot, select Sauté; adjust to normal. Heat coconut oil in Instant Pot. Add broccoli, onions, paprika, and salt; cook 8 to 10 minutes, stirring occasionally, until thoroughly cooked. Select Cancel.

Stir in tomatoes, black beans, chills, and water. Secure lid set pressure valve to Sealing. Select Manual, cook on High pressure 5 minutes. Select Cancel. Keep the pressure valve in the Sealing position to release pressure naturally.

Nutrition:

Calories 408, Total Fat 5. 3g, Saturated Fat 3. 4g, Cholesterol 0mg, Sodium 607mg, Total Carbohydrate 70. 7g, Dietary Fiber 18. 1g, Total Sugars 6g, Protein 23. 3g

21. Potato and Chickpea Curry

Preparation Time: 05 minutes | **Cooking Time:** 10 minutes | **Servings:** 2

Ingredients:

½ tablespoon coconut oil 1 small onion chopped

2 teaspoons paprika ½ teaspoon garlic powder

¼ teaspoon salt ¼ teaspoon chipotle chili powder

¼ teaspoon ground cumin 1 cup vegetable broth

1 cup chickpea rinsed and drained

¼ cup potatoes peeled and cut into 1/2-inch pieces

½ cup diced tomatoes

Directions:

Press Sauté, heat coconut oil in Instant Pot. Add chopped onions; cook 3 minutes or until softened. Add paprika, garlic powder, salt, chipotle chili powder, and ground cumin; cook and stir for 1 minute. Stir in broth, scraping up browned bits from the bottom of Instant Pot. Add chickpea, potatoes, and diced tomatoes; mix well.

Secure lid and move pressure release valve to the Sealing position. Press Manual or Pressure Cook; cook at High Pressure for 4 minutes.

When cooking is complete, press Cancel and use Quick-release. Press Sauté; cook and stir for 3 to 5 minutes or until thickened to desired consistency. Serve with desired toppings.

Nutrition:

Calories 575, Total Fat 11. 3g, Saturated Fat 3. 8g, Cholesterol 0mg, Sodium 679mg, Total Carbohydrate 96. 2g, Dietary Fiber 25. 1g, Total Sugars 13. 8g, Protein 26. 7g

Chapter 4: Soups and Stews

22. Cottage Cheese Soup

Preparation Time: 10 minutes | **Cooking Time:** 35 minutes | **Servings:** 2

Ingredients:

1 stalks leek, diced

1 tablespoon bell pepper, diced

¼ cup Swiss chard, sliced into strips

1/8 cup fresh kale

1 eggplant

½ tablespoon avocado oil

1/8 cup button mushrooms, diced

1 small onion, diced

½ cup cottage cheese

2 cups vegetable broth

1 bay leaf ½ teaspoon salt

¼ teaspoon garlic, minced 1/8 teaspoon paprika

Directions:

Place leek, bell pepper, Swiss chard, eggplant, and kale into a medium bowl, set aside in a separate medium bowl.

Press the Sauté button and add the avocado oil to Instant Pot. Once the oil is hot, add mushrooms and onion. Sauté for 4–6 minutes until the onion is translucent and fragrant.

Add leek, bell pepper, Swiss chard, and kale to Instant Pot. Cook for an additional 4 minutes. Press the Cancel button.

Add diced cottage cheese, broth, bay leaf, and seasonings to Instant Pot. Click the lid closed. Press the Soup button and set the time for 20 minutes.

When the timer beeps, allow a 10-minute natural release and quickly release the remaining pressure. Add eggplant on Keep Warm mode and cook for additional 10 minutes or until tender. Serve warm.

Nutrition:

Calories 212, Total Fat 3. 6g, Saturated Fat 1. 2g, Cholesterol 5mg, Sodium 1603mg, Total Carbohydrate 30. 7g, Dietary Fiber 11. 9g, Total Sugars 12. 7g, Protein 17g

23. Fresh Corn & Red Pepper Stew

Preparation Time: 15 minutes | **Cooking Time:** 30 minutes | **Servings:** 2

Ingredients:

1 teaspoon coconut oil ¼ cup sweet onion, chopped,

1 1/2 cups fresh corn kernels

1 teaspoon garlic, minced 2 cups vegetable broth,

¼ teaspoon salt 1/8 cup coconut cream

½ tablespoon cornmeal

½ small red bell pepper, diced Enough water

Directions:

Select the Sauté setting on the Instant Pot and heat the coconut oil. Add the onion, garlic, and salt and sauté for about 5 minutes, until the onion has softened and is translucent.

Add the fresh corn, broth, water, bell pepper, and stir well. Lock lid and set the Pressure Release to Sealing. Press the Cancel button to reset the cooking program, then select the Soup/Broth setting and set the cooking time for 15 minutes at High Pressure.

Meanwhile add water, coconut cream, and cornmeal.

Let the pressure release naturally for at least 10 minutes, then move the Steam Release to Vent to release any remaining steam.

Open the pot and stir in the cornmeal mixer into soup, then taste and adjust the seasoning with salt if needed.

Nutrition:

Calories 183, Total Fat 8. 3g, Saturated Fat 5. 7g, Cholesterol 0mg, Sodium 1070mg, Total Carbohydrate 21. 8g, Dietary Fiber 3. 3g, Total Sugars 5. 8g, Protein 8. 4g

24. Zucchini & White Bean Stew

Preparation Time:10 minutes | **Cooking Time:** 35 minutes | **Servings:** 2

Ingredients:

¼ ounce mushrooms

1 cup hot water

½ large zucchini

1 tablespoon coconut oil, divided

1 small onion, thinly sliced

½ teaspoon garlic powder

¼ teaspoons dried basil, crumbled

1 small (1-inch) cinnamon stick

¼ teaspoon salt

1/8 teaspoon freshly ground pepper

1 bay leaf

2 cups vegetable broth

¼ cup dried white beans, rinsed and soaked overnight and drained

1 tomato

¼ cup finely chopped fresh cilantro

Directions:

Select the Sauté setting on the Instant Pot and heat ¼ tablespoon coconut oil. Add zucchini and roast it and keep aside.

Add remaining coconut oil, add onion and sauté for about 5 minutes, until the onion has softened and is translucent. Add garlic powder, basil, cinnamon stick, salt, pepper, bay leaf, and the chopped mushrooms cook, stirring, for 1 minute add vegetable broth and add white beans and roast zucchini.

Lock lid and set the Pressure Release to Sealing. Press the Cancel button to reset the cooking program, then select the Soup/Broth setting and set the cooking time for 25 minutes at High Pressure.

Let the pressure release naturally for at least 10 minutes, then move the Steam Release to Vent to release any remaining steam.

Open the pot and remove the cinnamon stick and bay leaf. Stir in tomatoes and cilantro.

Nutrition:

Calories 210, Total Fat 7. 5g, Saturated Fat 6g, Cholesterol 0mg, Sodium 307mg, Total Carbohydrate 30. 9g, Dietary Fiber 11. 1g, Total Sugars 8g, Protein 8. 5g

25. Potato Tofu Soup

Preparation Time:10 minutes | **Cooking Time:** 35 minutes | **Servings:** 2

Ingredients:

½ tablespoon olive oil ½ celery cleaned and sliced

½ teaspoon garlic powder

1 sweet potato peeled and cut into 2-inch cubes

½ large potato peeled and cut into 2-inch cubes

½ cup tofu 2 cups vegetable broth

Juice from one lemon A handful of chopped parsley

Salt and pepper

Directions:

Hit the Sauté button and when it's hot, heat the olive oil in your Instant Pot and sauté the celery and garlic powder until they soften down, stirring often.

Add in the potatoes, sweet potatoes, tofu, broth, salt, and pepper, and stir well.

Lock lid, make sure the vent is sealed, and program for 6 minutes on High Pressure. You can do a Quick-release if you like or leave it to release on its own with soup like this it doesn't matter.

Once the pressure is released, open the lid and throw in the parsley and add the lemon juice.

Nutrition:

Calories 216, Total Fat 7. 6g, Saturated Fat 1. 5g, Cholesterol 0mg, Sodium 809mg, Total Carbohydrate 27. 2g, Dietary Fiber 3. 6g, Total Sugars 5. 2g, Protein 12. 2g

26. Tomato Gazpacho

Preparation Time: 2 Hours 25 minutes | **Cooking Time:** 15-60 minutes | **Servings:** 6

Ingredients:

2 Tablespoons + 1 Teaspoon Red Wine Vinegar, Divided

½ Teaspoon Pepper 1 Teaspoon Sea Salt

1 Avocado,

¼ Cup Basil, Fresh & Chopped

3 Tablespoons + 2 Teaspoons Olive Oil, Divided

1 Clove Garlic, crushed 1 Red Bell Pepper, Sliced & Seeded 1 Cucumber, Chunked

2 ½ lbs. Large Tomatoes, Cored & Chopped

Directions:

Place half of your cucumber, bell pepper, and ¼ cup of each tomato in a bowl, covering. Set it in the fridge.

Puree your remaining tomatoes, cucumber, and bell pepper with garlic, three tablespoons oil, two tablespoons of vinegar, sea salt, and black pepper into a blender, blending until smooth. Transfer it to a bowl, and chill for two hours.

Chop the avocado, adding it to your chopped vegetables, adding your remaining oil, vinegar, salt, pepper, and basil.

Ladle your tomato puree mixture into bowls, and serve with chopped vegetables as a salad.

Interesting Facts:

Avocados themselves are ranked within the top five of the healthiest foods on the planet, so you know that the oil that is produced from them is too. It is loaded with healthy fats and essential fatty acids. Like race bran oil it is perfect to cook with as well! Bonus: Helps in the prevention of diabetes and lowers cholesterol levels.

Nutrition:

Calories 70; Fat 2.7 g; Carbohydrates 13.8 g; Sugar 6.3 g; Protein 1.9 g; Cholesterol 0 mg

27.   Tomato Pumpkin Soup

Preparation Time: 25 minutes | **Cooking Time:** 15-60 minutes | **Servings:** 4

Ingredients:

2 cups pumpkin, diced

1/2 cup tomato, chopped

1/2 cup onion, chopped

1 1/2 tsp curry powder

1/2 tsp paprika

2 cups vegetable stock

1 tsp olive oil

1/2 tsp garlic, minced

Directions:

In a saucepan, add oil, garlic, and onion and sauté for 3 minutes over medium heat.

Add remaining ingredients into the saucepan and bring to boil.

Reduce heat and cover and simmer for 10 minutes.

Puree the soup using a blender until smooth.

Stir well and serve warm.

Nutrition:

Calories 70; Fat 2.7 g; Carbohydrates 13.8 g; Sugar 6.3 g; Protein 1.9 g; Cholesterol 0 mg

Chapter 5: Snacks

28. Thai Snack Mix

Preparation Time: 15 minutes | **Cooking Time:** 90 minutes | **Servings:** 4

Ingredients:

5 cups mixed nuts

1 cup chopped dried pineapple

1 cup pumpkin seed

1 teaspoon garlic powder

1 teaspoon onion powder

2 teaspoons paprika

1 teaspoon of sea salt

1/4 cup coconut sugar

1/2 teaspoon red chili powder

1/2 teaspoon ground black pepper

1 tablespoon red pepper flakes

1/2 tablespoon red curry powder

2 tablespoons soy sauce

2 tablespoons coconut oil

Directions:

Switch on the slow cooker, add all the ingredients in it except for dried pineapple and red pepper flakes, stir until combined, and cook for 90 minutes at a high heat setting, stirring every 30 minutes.

When done, spread the nut mixture on a baking sheet lined with parchment paper and let it cool.

Then spread dried pineapple on top, sprinkle with red pepper flakes and serve.

Nutrition:

Calories: 230 Cal Fat: 17.5 g Carbs: 11.5 g Protein: 6.5 g

Fiber: 2 g

29. Zucchini Fritters

Preparation Time: 10 minutes | **Cooking Time:** 6 minutes | **Servings:** 12

Ingredients:

1/2 cup quinoa flour

3 1/2 cups shredded zucchini

1/2 cup chopped scallions

1/3 teaspoon ground black pepper

1 teaspoon salt

2 tablespoons coconut oil

2 flax eggs

Directions:

Squeeze moisture from the zucchini by wrapping it in a cheesecloth and then transfer it to a bowl.

Add remaining ingredients, except for oil, stir until combined, and then shape the mixture into twelve patties.

Take a skillet pan, place it over medium-high heat, add oil and when hot, add patties and cook for 3 minutes per side until brown.

Serve the patties with your favorite vegan sauce.

Nutrition:

Calories: 37 Cal Fat: 1 g Carbs: 4 g Protein: 2 g Fiber: 1 g

30. Zucchini Chips

Preparation: 10 min | **Cooking:** 120 min | **Servings:** 4

Ingredients:

1 large zucchini, thinly sliced 1 teaspoon salt

2 tablespoons olive oil

Directions:

Pat dry zucchini slices and then spread them in an even layer on a baking sheet lined with parchment sheet.

Whisk together salt and oil, brush this mixture over zucchini slices on both sides and then bake for 2 hours or more until brown and crispy.

When done, let the chips cool for 10 minutes and then serve straight away.

Nutrition:

Calories: 54 Cal Fat: 5 g Carbs: 1 g Protein: 0 g

31.   Rosemary Beet Chips

Preparation Time: 10 minutes | **Cooking Time:** 20 minutes | **Servings:** 3

Ingredients:

3 large beets, scrubbed, thinly sliced

1/8 teaspoon ground black pepper

¼ teaspoon of sea salt

3 sprigs of rosemary, leaves chopped

4 tablespoons olive oil

Directions:

Spread beet slices in a single layer between two large baking sheets, brush the slices with oil, then season with spices and rosemary, toss until well coated, and bake for 20 minutes at 375 degrees F until crispy, turning halfway.

When done, let the chips cool for 10 minutes and then serve.

Nutrition:

Calories: 79 Cal Fat: 4.7 g Carbs: 8.6 g Protein: 1.5 g Fiber: 2.5 g

32. Quinoa Broccoli Tots

Preparation Time: 10 minutes | **Cooking Time:** 20 minutes | **Servings:** 16

Ingredients:

2 tablespoons quinoa flour

2 cups steamed and chopped broccoli florets

1/2 cup nutritional yeast

1 teaspoon garlic powder

1 teaspoon miso paste

2 flax eggs

2 tablespoons hummus

Directions:

Place all the ingredients in a bowl, stir until well combined, and then shape the mixture into sixteen small balls.

Arrange the balls on a baking sheet lined with parchment paper, spray with oil and bake at 400 degrees F for 20 minutes until brown, turning halfway. When done, let the tots cool for 10 minutes and then serve straight away.

Nutrition:

Calories: 19 Cal Fat: 0 g Carbs: 2 g Protein: 1 g Fiber: 0.5 g

Chapter 6: Desserts

33. Chocolate Watermelon Cups

Preparation Time: 2 hours | **Cooking Time:** 0 minutes

| **Servings:** 4

Ingredients:

2 cups watermelon, peeled and cubed

1 tablespoon stevia

1 cup coconut cream

1 tablespoon cocoa powder

1 tablespoon mint, chopped

Directions:

In a blender, combine the watermelon with the stevia and the other ingredients, pulse well, divide into cups and keep in the fridge for 2 hours before serving.

Nutrition:

Calories 164, Fat 14.6, Fiber 2.1, Carbs 9.9, Protein 2.1

34. Vanilla Raspberries Mix

Preparation Time: 10 minutes | **Cooking Time:** 10 minutes | **Servings:** 4

Ingredients:

1 cup of water

1 cup raspberries

3 tablespoons stevia

1 teaspoon nutmeg, ground

½ teaspoon vanilla extract

Directions:

In a pan, combine the raspberries with the water and the other ingredients, toss, cook over medium heat for 10 minutes, divide into bowls and serve.

Nutrition:

Calories 20, Fat 0.4, Fiber 2.1, Carbs 4, Protein 0.4

35. Ginger Cream

Preparation Time: 10 minutes | **Cooking Time:** 10 minutes | **Servings:** 4

Ingredients:

2 tablespoons stevia

2 cups coconut cream

1 teaspoon vanilla extract

1 tablespoon cinnamon powder

¼ tablespoon ginger, grated

Directions:

In a pan, combine the cream with the stevia and other ingredients, stir, cook over medium heat for 10 minutes, divide into bowls and serve cold.

Nutrition:

Calories 280, Fat 28.6, Fiber 2.7, Carbs 7, Protein 2.8

36. Chocolate Ginger Cookies

Preparation Time: 10 minutes | **Cooking Time:** 20 minutes | **Servings:** 6

Ingredients:

2 cups almonds, chopped

2 tablespoons flaxseed mixed with 3 tablespoons water

¼ cup avocado oil

2 tablespoons stevia

¼ cup of cocoa powder

1 teaspoon baking soda

Directions:

In your food processor, combine the almonds with the flaxseed mix and the other ingredients, pulse well, scoop tablespoons out of this mix, arrange them on a lined baking sheet, flatten them a bit and cook at 360 degrees F for 20 minutes.

Serve the cookies cold.

Nutrition:

Calories 252, Fat 41.6, Fiber 6.5, Carbs 11.7, Protein 3

37. Mint Cookies

Preparation Time: 10 minutes | **Cooking Time:** 20 minutes | **Servings:** 6

Ingredients:

2 cups coconut flour

3 tablespoons flaxseed mixed with 4 tablespoons water

½ cup coconut cream

½ cup coconut oil, melted

3 tablespoons stevia

2 teaspoons mint, dried

2 teaspoons baking soda

Directions:

In a bowl, mix the coconut flour with the flaxseed, coconut cream, and the other ingredients, and whisk well.

Shape balls out of this mix, place them on a lined baking sheet, flatten them, introduce them in the oven at 370 degrees F and bake for 20 minutes.

Serve the cookies cold.

Nutrition:

Calories 190, Fat 7.32, Fiber 2.2, Carbs 4, Protein 3

38.   Simple Almond Butter Fudge

Preparation: 15 minutes | **Cooking:** 0 | **Servings:** 8

Ingredients:

1/2 cup almond butter 15 drops liquid stevia

2 1/2 tbsp coconut oil

Directions:

Combine almond butter and coconut oil in a saucepan.

Gently warm until melted. Add stevia and stir well.

Pour mixture into the candy container and place in the

refrigerator until set. Serve and enjoy.

Nutrition:

Calories: 198 Total Carbohydrate: 5 g Cholesterol: 12

mg Total Fat: 10 g Fiber: 2 g Protein: 6 g Sodium: 257

mg

39. Quick Chocó Brownie

Preparation: 10 minutes | **Cooking:** 2 | **Servings:** 1

Ingredients:

1/4 cup almond milk 1 tbsp cocoa powder

1 scoop chocolate protein powder   1/2 tsp baking powder

Directions:

In a microwave-safe mug blend together baking powder, protein powder, and cocoa. Add almond milk to the mug and stir well. Place the mug in the microwave and microwave for 30 seconds. Serve and enjoy.

Nutrition:

Calories: 231 Total Carbohydrate: 2 g Cholesterol: 13 mg Total Fat: 15 g Fiber: 2 g Protein: 8 g Sodium: 298 mg

Chapter 7: Drinks

40. Thai Iced Tea

Preparation Time: 5 minutes | **Cooking Time:** 10 minutes | **Servings:** 4

Ingredients:

4 cups of water

1 can of light coconut milk (14 oz.)

¼ cup of maple syrup

¼ cup of muscovado sugar

1 teaspoon of vanilla extract

2 tablespoons of loose-leaf black tea

Directions:

In a large saucepan, over medium heat bring the water to a boil.

Turn off the heat and add in the tea, cover and let steep for five minutes.

Strain the tea into a bowl or jug. Add the maple syrup, muscovado sugar, and vanilla extract. Give it a good whisk to blend all the ingredients.

Set in the refrigerator to chill. Upon serving, pour ¾ of the tea into each glass, top with coconut milk, and stir.

Tips:

Add a shot of dark rum to turn this iced tea into a cocktail.

You could substitute the coconut milk for almond or rice

milk too.

Nutrition:

Calories 844 Carbohydrates: 2.3g Protein: 21.6g Fat:

83.1g

41. Hot Chocolate

Preparation Time: 5 minutes | **Cooking Time:** 15 minutes | **Servings:** 2

Ingredients:

Pinch of brown sugar

2 cups of milk, soy or almond, unsweetened

2 tablespoons of cocoa powder

½ cup of vegan chocolate

Directions:

In a medium saucepan, over medium heat gently bring the milk to a boil. Whisk in the cocoa powder.

Remove from the heat, add a pinch of sugar and chocolate. Give it a good stir until smooth, serve, and enjoy.

Tips:

You may substitute the almond or soy milk for coconut milk too.

Nutrition:

Calories 452 Carbs: 29.8g Protein: 15.2g Fat: 30.2g

42. Chai and Chocolate Milkshake

Preparation Time: 5 minutes | **Cooking Time:** 15 minutes | **Servings:** 2 servings

Ingredients:

1 and ½ cups of almond milk, sweetened or unsweetened

3 bananas, peeled and frozen 12 hours before use

4 dates, pitted

1 and ½ teaspoons of chocolate powder, sweetened or unsweetened

½ teaspoon of vanilla extract

½ teaspoon of cinnamon

¼ teaspoon of ground ginger

Pinch of ground cardamom

Pinch of ground cloves

Pinch of ground nutmeg

½ cup of ice cubes

Directions:

Add all the ingredients to a blender except for the ice-cubes. Pulse until smooth and creamy, add the ice-cubes, pulse a few more times and serve.

Tips:

The dates provide enough sweetness to the recipe, however, you are welcome to add maple syrup or honey for a sweeter drink.

Nutrition:

Calories 452 Carbs: 29.8g Protein: 15.2g Fat: 30.2g

Chapter 8: Dressings, Dips, and Sauces

43. Balsamic Vinaigrette

Preparation Time: 5 minutes | **Cooking Time:** 8 minutes | **Servings:** 1 cup

Ingredients:

Black pepper, one quarter teaspoon

Salt, one quarter teaspoon

Garlic powder, one quarter teaspoon

Agave nectar, one tablespoon

Dijon mustard, one tablespoon

Balsamic vinegar, one quarter cup

Olive oil, one half cup

Directions:

Mix well in a blender or a shaker jar.

Nutrition:

Calories: 91 Fat: 0.3 Fiber: 1.5 Carbs: 0.4 Protein: 0.4

44.   Chipotle Lime Dressing

Preparation Time: 5 minutes | **Cooking Time:** 8 minutes | **Servings:** 1 cup

Ingredients:

Garlic powder, one quarter teaspoon

Paprika, one quarter teaspoon

Agave nectar, one tablespoon

Red pepper, one chopped

Lime juice, three tablespoons

Vegenaise, three tablespoons

Directions:

Mix well in a shaker jar or a blender.

Nutrition:

Calories: 32 Fat: 0.3 Fiber: 1.5 Carbs: 0.4 Protein: 0.4

45. Sweet Mango and Orange Dressing

Preparation Time: 5 minutes | **Cooking Time:** 0 minutes | **Servings:** 1

Ingredients:

1 cup (165 g) diced mango, thawed if frozen

½ cup of orange juice

2 tablespoons rice vinegar

2 tablespoons fresh lime juice

¼ teaspoon salt (optional)

1 teaspoon date sugar (optional)

2 tablespoons chopped cilantro

Directions:

Pulse all the ingredients except for the cilantro in a food processor until it reaches the consistency you like. Add the cilantro and whisk well.

Store in an airtight container in the fridge for up to 2 days.

Nutrition:

Calories: 32 Fat: 0.1g Carbs: 7.4g Protein: 0.3g Fiber: 0.5g

Chapter 9: Bonus Recipes

46. Aubergine And Tomato Rogan Josh

Preparation Time: 5 minutes | **Cooking Time:** 15 minutes | **Servings:** 2

Ingredients:

1 tablespoon olive oil

1 shallot, chopped

2 cloves garlic, minced

2 teaspoons Rogan Josh spice paste or garam masala

2 big ripe tomatoes, chopped

1 large aubergine, chopped

½ cup of water

salt and pepper to taste

Juice from ½ lemon

½ cup pistachios shelled

1 bunch fresh coriander

Directions:

Press the Sauté button on the Instant Pot and heat the olive oil.

Sauté the shallot and garlic for 30 seconds or until fragrant.

Toast the garam masala or Rogan Josh spice paste for a minute until fragrant.

Add in the tomatoes and stir for 3 minutes.

Stir in the aubergine and water. Season with salt and pepper to taste. Drizzle with lemon juice.

Close the lid and set the vent to the Sealing position.

Press the Pressure Cook or Manual button and adjust the cooking time to 8 minutes.

Do natural pressure release.

Once the lid is open, stir in the pistachios and coriander.

Nutrition:

Calories 281, Total Fat 22g, Saturated Fat 3g, Total Carbs 19g, Net Carbs 14g, Protein 9g, Sugar: 3g, Fiber: 5g, Sodium: 53mg, Potassium:915mg, Phosphorus: 238mg

47.   Instant Pot Roasted Root Vegetables

Preparation Time: 5 minutes | **Cooking Time:** 5 hours | **Servings:** 6

Ingredients:

1-pound medium-sized potatoes, scrubbed and quartered

2 large carrots, peeled and roughly chopped

1 large parsnip, peeled and roughly chopped

1 bulb garlic, smashed

½ bunch fresh rosemary

3 tablespoons olive oil

salt and pepper to taste

Directions:

Place all ingredients in a mixing pot and toss to coat all ingredients with the oil and seasoning.

Place into the Instant Pot.

Close the lid but do not seal the vent.

Press the Slow Cook function and adjust the cooking time to 5 hours.

Halfway through the cooking time, carefully stir the vegetables for even browning.

Cook until done.

Nutrition:

Calories 144, Total Fat 7g, Saturated Fat 1g, Total Carbs 19g, Net Carbs 16g, Protein 2g, Sugar: 3g, Fiber: 3g, Sodium: 23mg, Potassium: 478mg, Phosphorus: 67mg

48.   Tomato Curry

Preparation Time: 5 minutes | **Cooking Time:** 15 minutes | **Servings:** 4

Ingredients:

2 tablespoons olive oil

4 cloves garlic, minced

1 1-inch ginger, sliced thinly

1 ½ pounds mixed tomatoes

A pinch of saffron

½ cup almond meal

2 fresh red chilis, chopped

5 curry leaves

1 tablespoon garam masala

1 14-ounce can coconut milk

2 teaspoon mango chutney (optional)

salt and pepper to taste

Directions:

Press the Sauté button on the Instant Pot and heat the oil.

Sauté the garlic and ginger until fragrant.

Stir in the tomatoes and saffron for 2 minutes.

Add in the rest of the ingredients.

Close the lid and set the vent to the Sealing position.

Press the Manual button and adjust the cooking time to 10 minutes.

Do natural pressure release.

Nutrition:

Calories 113, Total Fat 7g, Saturated Fat 1g, Total Carbs 11g, Net Carbs 8g, Protein 3g, Sugar: 3g, Fiber: 3g, Sodium: 176mg, Potassium: 625mg, Phosphorus:75 mg

49. Potato and Artichoke Al Forno

Preparation: 5 | **Cooking:** 5 hours | **Servings:** 5

Ingredients:

½ pound baby potatoes scrubbed clean 2 large fennel bulbs, peeled and sliced thinly 1 14-ounce artichoke hearts in oil 1 cup double cream Salt and pepper to taste

Directions:

Place all ingredients in the Instant Pot and give a good stir. Close the lid and do not seal the vent.

Press the Slow Cook button and adjust the cooking time to 5 hours. **Nutrition:**

Calories 258, Total Fat 16g, Saturated Fat 7g, Total Carbs 26g, Net Carbs 16g, Protein 6g, Sugar: 7g, Fiber: 10g, Sodium: 115mg, Potassium: 876mg, Phosphorus: 168mg

50. Mushroom Bourguignon

Preparation Time: 5 minutes | **Cooking Time:** 5 minutes | **Servings:** 6

Ingredients:

2 tablespoons olive oil

2 cloves garlic, minced

12 shallots, chopped

16 ounces dried porcini mushrooms, soaked in water overnight then drained

4 portobello mushrooms, sliced

16 ounces shiitake mushrooms, sliced

16 ounces chestnut mushrooms, sliced

1 medium carrot, sliced

1 sprig fresh thyme

2 bay leaves

1 cup red wine

2 tablespoons tomato paste Salt and pepper to taste

Directions:

Press the Sauté button on the Instant Pot and heat the oil.

Sauté the garlic and shallots until fragrant. Stir in the mushrooms and sauté for 3 minutes.

Add in the rest of the ingredients.

Close the lid and set the vent to the Sealing position.

Press the Pressure Cook or Manual button and adjust the cooking time to 5 minutes.

Do natural pressure release.

Nutrition:

Calories 346, Total Fat 6g, Saturated Fat 0.8g, Total Carbs 76g, Net Carbs 64g, Protein 12g, Sugar: 9g, Fiber: 12g, Sodium: 26mg, Potassium: 1662mg, Phosphorus: 337mg

Conclusion

There are so many powerful and persuasive reasons to make a positive change and switch over to a plant-based diet. A plant-based diet will improve your quality of life, give you more energy and vitality, help you lose unwanted body fat, and it may even lengthen your years on this beautiful planet. As a bonus, by making the change you will be making a real and significant difference to our planet Earth's future. So much energy and fossil fuels are wasted by sourcing meat and other animal products, transporting them from place to place across miles and miles of road, and processing all of these animal products.

By switching to a plant-based diet, you will be greatly decreasing your carbon footprint and ensuring that fewer animals have to suffer at the hands of humans. And isn't that a good feeling?